A Pet to the Vet

by Shirley Frederick
illustrated by Amanda Haley

Harcourt
Orlando Boston Dallas Chicago San Diego
Visit *The Learning Site!*
www.harcourtschool.com

I got a new pet.
His name is Chet.

My mom was busy
with the baby.

I was busy, too.
I took care of Chet.

Every day I took
Chet out for a walk.

Chet needed a shot.
My mom was busy.

So I took Chet
downtown to the vet.

The busy vet had
to take care of a cat.

Then the vet took
care of a brown duck.

Chet was not happy.
He got down and ran.

Chet does not need a shot. He does not need a vet.

Chet is just fine.
This pet does not
need a vet.